Contents

Editor	Billie Ciancio
Assistant Editors	Georgianne Detzner
	Irene Mueller
Religious Content Consultant	Reverend Elaine Petersen, M. Div.
Art Director	Janet Wilcox
Design	Matt Haak
Production Director	Art Steitz
Production Manager	Irene Zimmer
Vice President of Marketing & Sales	Stuart Hochwert
Newsstand Director	Toni Ballentine
Merchandise Manager	Lisa Behzad
Controller	Susan Lindahl
President & Publisher	Marie Clapper
Chairman of the Board	Lyle Clapper

The **Clapper Publishing** Family
• Pack-O-Fun®
• Crafts 'n Things®
• Painting™
• The Cross Stitcher®
• Bridal Crafts™

Library of Congress Catalog Number: 98-067796
ISBN: 0-9652041-1-1
Manufactured in the United States
First Printing 1998
©1998 by Pack-O-Fun, Inc. • 2400 Devon, Suite 375 • Des Plaines, IL 60018-4618

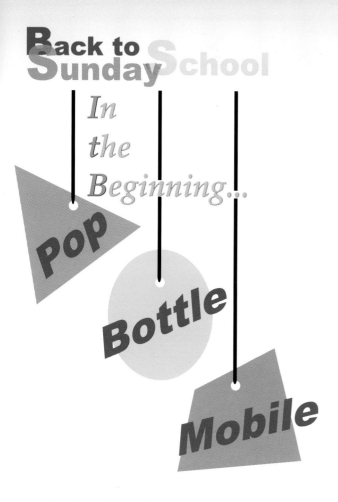

In the Beginning...

Pop Bottle Mobile

Here is a quick-and-easy way to make a Bible-theme mobile. The cooperation needed to make a class mobile can be a fun and effective way to help children get to know one another and develop class spirit as the church school year begins. Point out to the children that since the hanging elements of the mobile move as the air does, it is important that it be attractive when seen from all sides. Explain that they will be working in pairs or small groups to make one of the elements that hang from the mobile. We have printed basic mobile-making instructions below, followed by ideas for a Creation Mobile. We thought Creation was a good place to start! — but feel free to make your mobile represent any Bible theme you choose. For example, you could make one representing the 12 Sons of Jacob (Genesis 25: 22-26) or the Fruits of the Spirit (Galatians 5: 22-23).

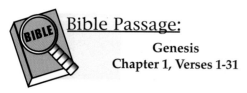

Bible Passage:

**Genesis
Chapter 1, Verses 1-31**

Materials

- One-gallon bleach or 2-liter pop bottle
- Black medium-line permanent marker
- Fishing line, ⅛" ribbon, or yarn
- Hole punch, scissors, ruler, fine sandpaper

Instructions

Note: Adult supervision is needed when poking a hole with scissors

1 **Make the base* of the mobile.** Measure and mark 4" down from top of bottle. Use point of scissors to punch a hole below marked line. Push one blade of scissors through hole and cut around the 4" line. Recycle bottom of bottle. Sand cut edge of base.

2 **Make the holes.** Count number of items you wish to hang from mobile. Mark that number of holes evenly-spaced around bottom of base. Use hole punch to make holes. If desired, use marker to write title on base describing theme of your mobile.

3 **Hang the theme elements.** Decide how long you would like each element of your mobile to hang from the base. Cut fishing line accordingly, leaving a little extra line for tying. Tie one end of each fishing line length onto each element of mobile. Tie other ends of each line into one of the holes around the base. To hang mobile, remove bottle cap. Cut 20" length of ⅛" ribbon. As you put bottle cap back on bottle, "catch" center of ribbon under cap. Tie ribbon ends in a knot. Hang mobile as desired.

* *We are using the term "base" to describe that part of mobile from which theme elements hang.*

Creation Mobile

Folded-Paper Sunburst
The first day of Creation: "Let there be light."

You will need two 8½" x 12" pieces of yellow construction paper, a black marker, glue, paper, pencil, ruler, and a hole punch. Draw a sunburst shape on yellow paper and cut out. Trace and cut three more sunbursts.

To finish the sunburst, fold each shape in half. See photo. Glue together as shown. Write verse on all sides. Punch hole in top. Hang on mobile.

Rainbow over the Ocean

The second day of Creation: "Let there be sky in the midst of the waters."

You will need blue construction paper, six 12" chenille stems: blue, purple, red, orange, yellow, and green, a black marker, glue, scissors, ruler, pencil, and three large paper clips.

To make the ocean, cut one 8" square from blue paper. Fold paper in half. See photo. Cut waves along unfolded long edges. Write verse on each side.

Figure 1

To make the rainbow, see Figure 1. Line up the ends of chenille stems in the following (rainbow) order: blue, purple, red, orange, yellow, green. Use one paper clip to hold ends together. Carefully begin bending stems into an arch. Secure at midpoint with another paper clip. Continue carefully bending stems until arch of rainbow is complete. Secure with third paper clip.

To hang rainbow over ocean, remove paper clip from one end of one rainbow. See photo. Glue end of rainbow on back of one set of ocean waves at the side edge as shown. Remove paper clip from other end of rainbow. Glue rainbow end on back of same set of ocean waves at the other end. Remove third paper clip. Glue two sets of waves together with rainbow ends sandwiched between them. Hang on mobile.

Traced-Hands Tree

The third day of Creation: "Let the earth bring forth grass ... and trees bearing fruit."

You will need white, green, and brown construction paper, two cotton balls, glue, crayons or markers, pencil, hole punch, and scissors.

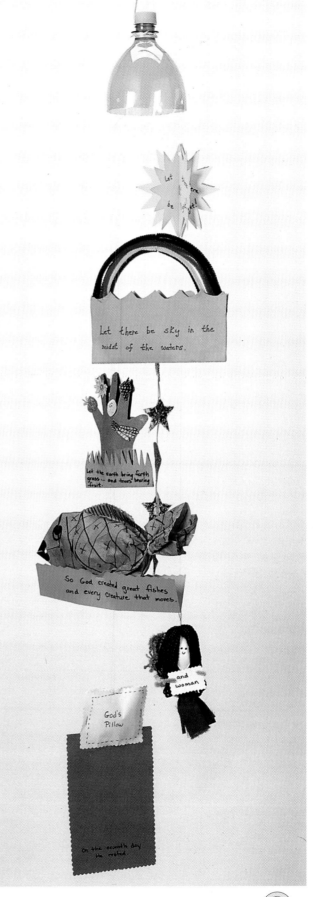

To make the tree, fold brown paper in half. Trace one hand on paper. Cut through both layers to make two hand shapes. To shape trunk, sandwich cotton between wrist and palm of hands. Glue together. For branches, leave fingers unglued on both sides of tree.

To decorate the tree, draw and color several pictures of flowers, fruits, seeds, and vegetables. Cut out and glue on both sides of tree. Fringe green paper for grass. Glue on bottom of both sides of tree. Write verse on grass. Punch hole through tops of tree's middle branches. Hang tree on mobile.

Heavenly Lights

The fourth day of creation: "Let there be lights in the sky of heaven..."

You will need white poster board, silver, gold, and blue glitter, one yellow paper clip, 18" of ¼" ribbon, glue, shoe-box lid, yellow jumbo craft stick, fishing line, black marker, paper, pencil, and scissors.

To make the Lights, trace and cut out patterns on page 41. Follow directions on patterns. Holding them over box lid to catch any stray glitter, glue glitter on both sides of shapes. See photo. Glue shapes along length of ribbon. Write *Let there be lights* on one side of craft stick and write *in the sky of heaven* on other side of craft stick. Fasten paper clip to center of craft stick. Tie end of ribbon through bottom loop of paper clip. Hang on mobile.

Paper-Bag Fish

Day five of Creation: "So God created great whales and every creature that moves."

Materials
• Brown lunch bag
• Newspaper
• Blue construction paper
• School / household glue
• Markers, pencil, rubber band

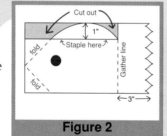

Figure 2

Instructions
1 Draw the fish shape. See Figure 2. Lay bag flat with open end toward the right. Use ruler and pencil to mark gather line 3" from open end, a horizontal line 1" down from the top, and fold lines at left corners as shown. Use pencil to draw fin shape. Use markers to draw eye and designs.

2 Shape the fish. Cut out fin shape. Staple fin closed. For fish nose, fold over and staple corners. To puff out body, crumble and stuff newspaper into bag opening.

3 Finish up. To form tail, use fingers to gather bag at gather line and rubber band to hold in place. For ocean, fold blue paper in half. Cut waves on long sides opposite fold. Write Bible verse on each side of ocean. Glue fish in ocean. Punch hole in top of fin. Hang fish on mobile.

Adam-and-Eve Spoon Dolls

The sixth day of Creation: "In the image of God he created man and woman."

You will need two plastic spoons, yarn, two 1½" x 7" strips of brown felt or fabric, one 2" x 6" piece of white cardboard, two 12" tan chenille stems, a black permanent marker, scissors, and a hole punch.

To make the clothing, fold each felt strip in half. For neck opening, cut a small slit centered along the fold. Slip clothing over spoons.

To make Adam and Eve's arms, cut one chenille stem in half. Wrap stem around top of spoon handle under clothing so arms extend from sides of clothing. For belt, wrap other stem piece around middle of clothing. Repeat for second figure. Use marker to draw facial features. Cut several 2"-3" strands of yarn. To make curly hair, unravel the strands. Glue strands around face to make hair, beard, and mustache.

To make the sign, write verse on both sides of cardboard. Glue Adam on one side of sign and Eve on the other. Punch hole in top of sign. Tie sign on mobile.

God's Bed

The seventh day of Creation: "On the seventh day he rested."

You will need purple and white construction paper, four cotton balls, black marker, glue, pinking shears or fancy paper-edgers, and ruler.

To make the bed, cut a 4" x 8" rectangle from purple paper for blanket. For pillow, cut two 3" x 4" rectangles from white paper. Write *God's Pillow* and draw stitch marks on one side of each paper pillow. Write verse on both sides of blanket. Glue cotton balls on back side of one paper pillow. Sandwich top 1½" of blanket between paper pillows and glue together. Punch hole in top of pillow. Hang bed on mobile.

Noah's Ark

by Connie Matricardi

Making this Noah's Ark project is a great way to help classmates get acquainted. Pair children up two-by-two to work on the animal pairs. If you're really ambitious and have the time, consider having the children research their animals - where they live now, what they eat, how they care for their babies, etc.

Materials

- One sheet each of craft foam: green, red, pink, purple, orange, yellow, white
- Two sheets of blue craft foam
- Three sheets of brown craft foam
- Scrap of peach craft foam
- Yarn scraps in choice of color
- Black fine-line permanent marker
- Craftfoam glue*
- Paper, pencil, scissors
- (Option: 1¼" tall miniature basket)

*Craftfoam Glue from Beacon™ Chemical Co. was used for this project. For more information see "Where To Find It" on page 48.

Instructions

1 **Trace and cut out patterns on page 42,43 and 44.** Follow directions on patterns.

2 **Make the ark.** (*Note: Follow manufacturer's directions for gluing.*) See Figure 1. Glue ark shapes together at sides. See photo. Glue roof shapes on each side of ark.

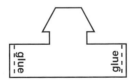

Figure 1

3 **Draw the ark.** (*Note: Draw front and back of each shape in the same way.*) See photo. Use marker to draw scalloped lines on roof. Draw door frames, shape of boat, wood lines, and portholes on ark.

4 **Finish the ark.** Glue wave shapes on each side of ark.

5 **Make the animals.** Glue each animal shape together at top of body (*Note: Legs must be allowed to separate so that animals can stand.*) See photo. Use marker to draw details on each side of animal. Glue ears on elephant where indicated by dashed line on pattern. For tails of animals, cut 2½" to 3" lengths from yarn scraps. Glue tails between animal shapes. Knot ends of tails except for lambs. For lambs, glue other end of tail between animal shapes.

6 **Make the doves.** Glue wings on doves. In the same way as animals, glue dove shapes together. Use marker to dot eyes. Perch doves on roof.

7 **Make Mr. and Mrs. Noah.** Glue top of body shapes together. See photo. Glue face, arms, and hands on each body. Use marker to draw details on faces and clothing. (*Option: See photo. Glue basket on Mrs. Noah.*)

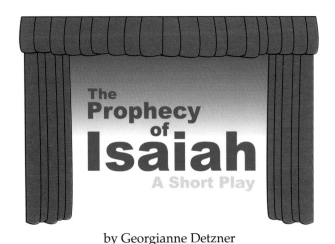

The Prophecy of Isaiah
A Short Play

by Georgianne Detzner

The Play:

Enter Isaiah.
Isaiah (the narrator): My name is Isaiah. I welcome you to our play. God has chosen me to preach his word. Listen now and watch.
Isaiah moves to left side of stage.
In a future time known only to God, a wonderful child will be born in the House of David.

Enter Joseph, carrying baby Jesus, and Mary.
Joseph: His name will be IMMANUEL . . .
Mary *taking the baby:* **which means "God is With Us".**
Joseph and Mary move stage right.

Enter five boys and girl dressed as shepherds and wearing sunglasses.
Shepherds: The people who have walked in darkness *remove sunglasses* **. . . will see a great light!**
Shepherds move next to Joseph and Mary.

Enter two children with Wolf and Lamb masks carrying pillows.
Wolf and Lamb: The wolf will lie down with the lamb!
They lay down on stage.

Enter two children with Calf and Lion masks, one carrying a large box of cookies.
Calf and Lion *eating from the box:* **The calf and the lion shall feed together!**

Enter a small child.
Small child: A little child shall lead them!
Small child motions to animals to get up. Wolf, Lamb, Calf, and Lion hold hands. Child takes wolf's paw and "leads" the animals to stand next to the shepherds.

Isaiah places two boxes on stage. One contains a cardboard sword, two flags, and a cardboard rifle. The other box is empty and has the symbol for NO on it.

Isaiah moves to the side and all characters join him in the middle of the stage, standing several feet behind the boxes.

One shepherd *comes forward and takes sword from box, shows it to audience, puts it in NO box:* **Swords shall be hammered into plowshares.**

Another shepherd *comes forward, takes flags from box, crosses and then uncrosses them in front of audience and then puts them in NO box:* **Nation shall not rise up against nation.**

A third shepherd *takes rifle from box, shoulders it, salutes, holds rifle up to audience, and then puts it in NO box:* **And there shall be no more training for war.**

All *stepping forward:* **The earth will be filled with the knowledge of God.**
All hold up a banner that says LOVE ONE ANOTHER.

THE END

Props:

Basic (No–Sew!) Costume

(for Isaiah, Mary, Joseph, the shepherds, and the little child)

Materials (for each)
• Two fabric remnants in colors and textures of choice
• Two yards of rope, twine, or fabric, cut in half
• Sweatshirt to match or coordinate with fabrics
• One pair thongs or sandals
• Scissors, tape measure

Simple costume; no sewing required!

Instructions

Note: Wear costume over jeans or sweatpants, sweatshirt, and sandals or thongs.

1 Make the gown. Measure child from shoulder to ankle and again around hips. Cut one fabric into a rectangle that measures twice first measurement long and one-and-a-half times hip measurement wide. Fold fabric length in half . Cut a slit along middle of fold wide enough for head to fit through. See drawing. Slip fabric over child's head. Use a length of robe or fabric to belt gown at waist.

2 Make the head piece. Cut second fabric remnant to measure about 36" x 48". See drawing. Center over head so face is showing. Tie rope or fabric around head to secure.

The Masks

Materials

- Four paper plates
- Acrylic paints: gray, tan, gold
- White poster board
- Gold crinkley gift-bag stuffing
- Three brown chenille stems
- White cotton balls
- ¼" elastic
- Black permanent marker
- Thick craft glue
- Scissors, pencil, stapler

Instructions

Note: No patterns are provided for the masks. See drawings for ear and muzzle shapes or design your own. Have children wear clothes in the colors of their masks. Sweatsuits in appropriate colors are ideal. Adult supervision is needed when using a stapler.

1 Make the wolf. On one paper plate, draw circles for eyes and cut out. Draw mouth with teeth and cut out. Cut out ears from poster board. Glue ears on plate. Paint mask gray. Let dry. Use marker to draw black nose.

2 Make the calf. Cut away bottom of plate. Cut ears and muzzle from poster board. Cut circles for eyes. Glue ears and muzzle on face. Paint mask tan. Let dry. Use marker to draw nostrils.

3 Make the lion. Cut away bottom of plate. Cut circles for eyes. For mane, glue bag stuffing around plate. For whiskers, cut chenille stems in half and glue on bottom of mask.

4 Make the lamb Cut away bottom of plate. Cut circles for eyes. Cut ears from poster board. Glue ears on head. For fur, glue cotton balls on face.

5 Finish the masks. Measure, cut, and staple elastic on masks to fit and secure around children's heads.

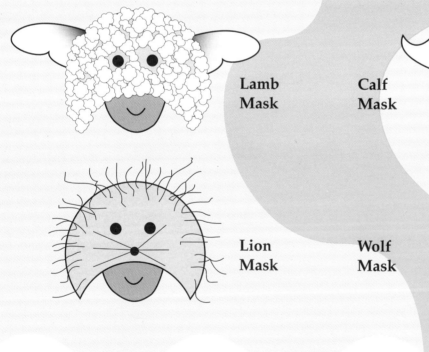

Lamb Mask

Lion Mask

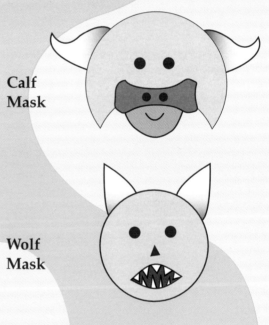

Calf Mask

Wolf Mask

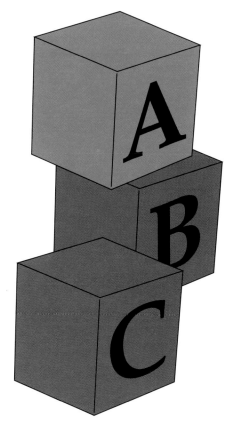

Narrator: **We've studied the Bible… Old Testament and New, and what we have learned, we will now share with you.**

1st child (*flipping letter out from behind back*): **C. CHRIST is my personal Saviour.**

2nd child: **H. When I think of Jesus, I feel HAPPY.**

3rd child: **R. He is RISEN.**

4th: **I. IN the beginning, God created the heaven and the earth.**

5th: **S. God So loved the world that He gave his only begotten SON.**

6th: **T. The Angel said, "Fear not, for behold, I bring you good TIDINGS of great joy."**

7th: **I. The Lord said, "I am the beginning and the end."**

8th: **A. ADAM was the first man.**

9th: **N. Love thy NEIGHBOR as thyself.**

10th: **L. Consider the LILIES of the field; they toil not, neither do they spin.**

11th: **O. Seek and ye shall find; knock and it shall be OPENED for you.**

12th: **V. Do not take the name of the Lord in VAIN.**

13th: **E. Believe in Christ and you'll have life ETERNAL.**

Narrator (*Walking to center of line, separating words "Christian" and "Love" with a blank card*): **We've learned lots of facts – that's easy to see – But our newly learned FAVORITE is…**

All: **JESUS LOVES ME!**
(*All 14 children flip their cards over. The line no longer reads "Christian Love" but instead reads "Jesus Loves Me."*)

An easy-to-learn presentation for Sunday school or Bible school.

This skit requires 14 children. Each holds a card which has one letter on the front and another on the back. Each child recites a line which goes with the letter on the front of the card. But if you are working with more than 14 children for your program, some kids can be card holders and others line reciters. It's possible to work with fewer than 14 if some kids can double up and hold 2 cards each.

The children stand in a straight line and hold cards behind their backs until each says his line. Then the card comes forward, and words are recited with capitalized word accented. The Narrator's role is slightly different from the others. His first lines are delivered without a card and letter.

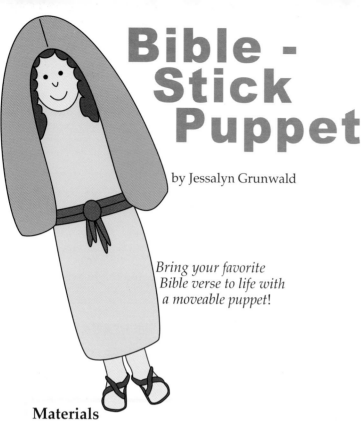

Bible - Stick Puppet

by Jessalyn Grunwald

*Bring your favorite
Bible verse to life with
a moveable puppet!*

Materials

- White poster board
- Poster paints: blue, brown, red, white.
- Black marker
- Four paper brads
- Six craft sticks
- Tissue paper (optional)
- Yarn (optional)
- Thick craft glue
- Paper, paper punch, pencil, scissors

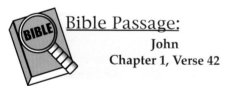

Bible Passage:
John
Chapter 1, Verse 42

Instructions

1 **Trace and cut out patterns on page 45.** Follow directions on patterns. With paper punch (or tip of pencil) make holes in patterns.

2 **Put together and paint puppet.** See photo. Fasten puppet together with brads as shown. Draw in facial features with markers. Paint hair, beard, and clothing. Add yarn hair and/or a tissue paper veil if desired. *Quick Tip: To make curly hair, gently pull apart yarn strands.*

3 **Finish up.** Glue two craft sticks together three times. Glue one "long" stick on back of body and one on back of each hand.

Papier Mâché Puppets

P apier mâché is a wonderful technique for making Bible story figures or puppets. Children generally enjoy the process and the results are very rewarding! You may wish to teach your students to make paper mâché figures to represent a Bible story like the Nativity grouping we show here. Or, you may wish to have them make puppets to act out a favorite Bible story. You will need four days to complete your Bible figures or five days to make the Bible puppets and practice your play.

To prepare your group for puppet-making, first choose a Bible story or stories that they want to act out. Some suggestions are: "Joseph and the Coat of Many Colors," "David and Goliath," "The Good Samaritan," and "The Christmas Story."

Next, decide if everyone in the group will be in the same play, or if the group will be divided to act out several plays. Familiarize the children with the story by telling or reading it several times.

Now you are ready to discuss the characters. You may have to "invent" a few new ones so each child has a part (for example, the innkeeper at Bethlehem may have a wife who nags him to find a space for Mary and Joseph.)

Finally, after all the characters have been chosen or assigned, the children are ready to begin building their puppets!

Materials

To make puppet:
- One 2" section of toilet paper roll
- Two pieces of 12" x 14" fabric

To make figure:
- One 20oz., 30 oz., or 48 oz. beverage bottle

Needed for both:
- One 3" foam ball
- 50 *torn* ½" x 4" newspaper strips
- 15-20 *torn* 1" x 4" paper toweling strips
- Acrylic paints: colors for face, facial features, and figure costumes
- Hair materials: yarn, fur, fiberfill, doll hair, or shredded paper
- Costume embellishments: buttons, beads from old jewelry, ribbon, felt scraps
- Flour
- Water
- Thick craft glue
- One large empty margarine tub or similar
- Metal whisk
- Needle**, straight pins, thread, rubber band, scissors, metal spoon, mixing spoon, paper towels, aluminum foil, newspapers, paper, pencil, large plastic bowl.

* Styrofoam® brand foam balls from the Dow Chemical Company were used for this project.
**Candlewicking needles work well for beginning stitchers.

Day 1

1 Make the form for the puppet or figure. (Can be done ahead of time by leader.) For the puppet, gently push cardboard tube into foam ball. To make more room for fingers, use metal spoon to carve out a small amount of foam from inside the tube. For the figure, remove and recycle bottle cap. Gently push foam ball onto bottle neck using twisting motion.

2 Make the papier mâché. In large bowl, combine equal parts flour and water. Mix with a metal whisk or use hand to squeeze out lumps. Add several tablespoons of glue until consistency of heavy cream. (Papier mâché will thicken.) Add more flour or water if necessary. Keep covered in refrigerator until ready to use (will last for a few days). When ready to use, pour mixture for each child into margarine containers.

Figure 1

3 Papier Mâché the figure or puppet head. Cover work area with newspaper. Dip a newspaper strip in papier mâché. See Figure 1. Gently "wring" the strip out with fingers. See Figure 2. Completely cover head and neck or head, neck, and body with several layers of newspaper strips placing them in all directions as shown. Try to keep strips smooth.

Figure 2

4 Dry the papier mâché. On a sunny day, set puppet heads out in sunlight. In humid weather, drying time will be longer. Damp heads can be placed in warm oven to speed drying process.

Group Tip: To avoid messy trips to the clean-up area for handwashing, provide several buckets of water and paper towels at work area.

Day 2

1 Apply the papier mâché. Cover work surface with newspaper. Using the same method used to attach newspaper strips, cover head and neck and figure's body with paper towel strips. (This makes puppet or figure stronger and gives a smooth, white surface for painting.)

2 Make the facial features. For nose, roll a piece of paper towel into a ball. Dip ball in papier mâché. Squeeze out excess and shape ball into a rough triangle-shape nose. Stick nose onto head. Attach nose with paper towel strips. (**DON'T SKIP THIS STEP**! Features will fall off if not secured with strips.) Use nose-making technique to add other features such as ears, chin, beard, eyebrows. Dry thoroughly.

Day 3

1 **Paint the faces**. Paint head and neck with skin color of choice. Let dry.

2 **Plan the costumes.** While faces are drying, discuss how costumes might look. (For example, a king might have an elegant look: aluminum foil crown, fancy fabric robe and jewels; a poor man might have torn, worn clothes with sewn or glued on patches.)

3 **Paint the features.** Use markers or acrylics to draw eyes, mouth, nose, cheeks, etc. Let dry.

Quick Tip: Use a hair dryer to speed paint drying time.

Day 4 — For puppet only!

1 **Trace and cut out pattern on page 47.** Follow directions on pattern. (Unless extra adult help is available, leader may want to do this step ahead of time. If children are doing this step, cut several patterns at once from newspaper.) Pin right sides of costume pieces together. See Figure 3. Use running stitches to sew costume seams as shown.

Figure 3

2 **Turn costume right side out.** Sew or glue on embellishments as desired. Apply glue generously to puppet neck. Insert neck into top opening of costume. Wrap rubber band around neck to hold costume in place.

Day 4 — For figure only!

1 Paint body using clothing color of choice. Let dry.

2 Here are some other costume suggestions:

- For angel's gown, cut a 12" circle from cloth. Cut a 1¾" circle in the center for the neck opening. To fit gown over angel's head, cut a 1" slit in the back. Slip gown over angel's head and glue in place around the neck. Glue choice trim around neck and bottom of gown.
- For wings, fold two 8" paper doilies in half. Glue on back of angel.
- For hair or beard, cut 4-ply yarn into 4" lengths. To curl hair, separate the yarn strands. Glue hair or beard on head.
- For halo, bend a metallic gold or silver chenille stem into a circle leaving a 3" tail. Fold tail down and glue on back of head.
- For king's crown, cut a 2½" x 9½" rectangle from metallic cardboard. Cut points along top edge. Glue sequins on crown.
- For veil or shepard's drape, cut a 9" x 16" piece of fabric. Fold one long side of fabric over 1½". Center and glue across top of head or use chenille stem folded into a circle to hold on head.
- For sheperd's hat, trace an 8" plate onto cloth. Use pinking shears to cut out circle. Center circle on top of head. Use chenille stem formed into a cirlce to hold hat on head.

Note: To make baby Jesus, use flesh-color paint to paint a 1½" foam ball for the head. For body, cut ½" from pointed end of 2" foam egg. Glue head on cut end of body. For bunting, use pinking shears to cut an 8" square of fabric. Wrap baby Jesus in bunting. Tie 18" of ¼" ribbon around bunting and tie in a bow in the front. Use a marker to paint sleeping eyes on the face. Fold 6" of metallic chenille stem into halo shape. Glue halo on head.

Day 5 — For puppet!

1 **Add the remaining details.** To give each puppet personality, add hair, beard, hat, cloak, veil, scar, mustache, etc.

2 **Prepare for the play.** Practice movements and voice of each character.

A Time for Thanks
Craft-Stick Trivet
by Karen Wiant

Bible Passage:
Colossians
Chapter 3, Verse 15

Materials
- Eight jumbo craft sticks
- Four clothes-pin doll stands
- Paint pens: orange, red, purple, blue, black
- Clear enamel
- Eraser, pencil, wood glue

Instructions

1 To paint the trivet, first seal both sides of the craft sticks with several coats of enamel. Let dry.

2 See photo. Use pencil to lightly sketch words and hearts on six of the craft sticks. Using photo as a guide, use paint pens to carefully trace over pencil lines (changing colors as shown).

3 Use red pen to paint the doll stands red. Let dry.

4 To assemble the trivet, see photo. To make the bottom supports, lay two undecorated sticks vertically and close together on work surface. Position decorated sticks horizontally in proper order on top of support sticks. Glue decorated sticks onto supports. Let dry. To attach the stands, turn trivet over and position one stand on each corner of base. Let dry.

Thanksgiving Tree

Let nature help you count your blessings!   by Pat Talsness

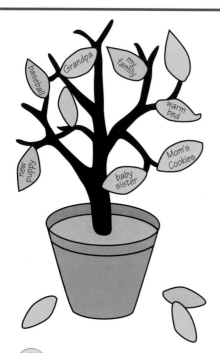

1 Several weeks before Thanksgiving, take a walk through your neighborhood or around your church and find one perfect branch for your tree. Bring it back and put it in an old flowerpot. Pour plaster of Paris in the pot to hold the branch in place.

2 Cut out lots of colorful paper leaves. Each night before bed or at the beginning of Sunday school, write one thing you are thankful for on a leaf, and hang it on the tree.
- By Thanksgiving, your tree will be filled with colorful reminders of all the blessings your family has received.

Advent

Even little fingers can "light" the flames!

Not-So-Hot Foam Advent Wreath

by Mary T. Cosgrove

Materials
- Craft foam: kelly green, purple, pink, yellow
- 9" plastic-canvas round
- Green artificial holly leaves (from a stemmed bush)
- Four white 12" chenille stems
- 2 yards of white ¼" ribbon
- Thick craft glue
- Craft-foam glue*
- Scissors, ruler, marking pen, wax paper

Craftfoam Glue from the Beacon Chemical Co. was used for this project. See "Where To Find It" on page 48.

1 **Trace and cut out pattern on page 41.** Follow directions on pattern. For candles, cut one pink and three purple 2½" x 4½" foam pieces. For base, cut a 3¾" circle from center of plastic-canvas round, leaving a ring 18-holes wide. Using plastic-canvas ring as a pattern, cut a slightly larger ring from green foam. Cut ribbon into four 18" lengths.

2 **Make the candles.** To make candle shape, fold pink foam piece so 4½" sides overlap ½". Following craft-foam glue manufacturer's instructions, glue overlapping edges. Repeat for three purple candles.

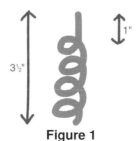

3½"   1"

Figure 1

3 **Make the wreath.** To make holes to hold candles, use bottoms of candles as patterns to trace four circles evenly spaced around foam ring. Cut out circles. Lay plastic-canvas ring on wax paper. Glue foam ring on top of plastic-canvas ring. Glue candles in cut-out places on wreath.

4 **Finish the wreath.** Overlap and glue leaves to cover top of wreath. See Figure 1. To make candle wicks, wrap each chenille stem around finger making four spiral shapes measuring 3½" including a 1" tail. Place one stem inside each candle so tail end sticks up to form wick. Tie a ribbon length in a bow around bottom of each candle. To "light" candles push a yellow flame into top of one candle each week in Advent, saving pink candle for fourth week.

Table Wreath

by Terrilynn Quillen

Bible Passage:

Luke
Chapter 1, Verses 26-33

Materials
- One 10″ round foil gas stove burner liner*
- Eight 20mm brass paper fasteners
- Four ¾″ x 1½″ miniature foil tea-candle holders
- 18″ of ½″ lavender grosgrain ribbon
- 6″ of ½″ pink grosgrain ribbon
- 16″ of wired pine garland
- Twelve 1½″ pine cones
- Four 1½″ x 2″ votive candles: one pink, three purple
- One 10″ pink paper plate
- Thick craft glue
- Scissors

*Option: Substitute a foil pie tin with center cut out for the burner liner.

Instructions
Note: Adult supervision is needed when lighting candles. Candles should be lit for only a short time and blown out when unattended.

1 **Prepare the liner and holders.** With point of scissors, poke eight holes, evenly spaced around the liner. Poke a hole in the bottom of each candle holder. Push a brad through each hole in liner so prongs extend on the top side. Place wreath on paper plate.

2 **Decorate the wreath.** Cut lavender ribbon into three 6″ lengths.

Glue pink ribbon and each lavender ribbon around the outside of a candle holder. Cut garland into four equal lengths. See photo. Attach garland and candle holders with brads as shown. Place candles in holders. Arrange pine cones in garland branches.

Did you know?

Before the celebrations of Hanukkah and Christmas began, ancient peoples honored Saturn, the god of agriculture, with a midwinter festival called Saturnalia.

Christmas Bells

Bell Ornament

by Laura Tomczyk

Here's a great project for families and community groups.

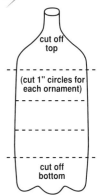

Figure 1

Materials:
- One clear plastic 1.25 liter soda bottle
- Two ¾" gold bells
- 32" length of ⅛" green satin ribbon
- 10" of metallic gold cord
- Green and gold glitter
- Thick craft glue
- Hole punch, scissors

Instructions

1 Cut off the top and bottom of the plastic bottle. See Figure 1. Cut 1" wide rings for each ornament. Punch 8 holes about 1" apart in the ring.

2 Choose one of the holes to be the top. See Figure 2. String the ribbon through the holes starting at top hole. When you reach the starting point, pull the ribbon through so there is a 2" tale. Insert the long end of the ribbon through the top hole, then go around the second side of the ring. When you get back to the top hole, tie two ends of ribbon into a bow.

3 Decorate the ring with glitter. String the bells onto the cord. Tie a knot, about 1 inch up. Then put the cord up through the center hole and tie a knot to hang.

Figure 2

Cream-Cup Bell Decorations

by Jeannine La Roche

Make beautiful bells from crafting leftovers!

Materials
- Cream cups
- Acrylic paints: choice of colors
- Glitter: choice of colors
- Cord, ribbon, or mini-garland: choice of colors
- Assorted trims
- Assorted embellishments: appliques, beads, bows.
- Thick craft glue
- Scissors, toothpick

Instructions

1 **Prepare the cups**. Thoroughly wash and dry cups. Paint inside and outside.

2 **Decorate the cups.** Use glue to cover outside surface of cup. Sprinkle on glitter. Glue on assorted trims and embellishments as desired.

3 **Make hanger.** Cut cord, ribbon, or mini-garland to desired length. Tie ends together in knot. Use toothpick to poke hole in top of cup. Use toothpick to push knot through hole. Glue knot in place.

Options:
- Use a small bead or jingle bell to make a bell clapper.
- String several cups together to make a swag or garland.
- Use other cup-shaped, recycled containers to make larger bells.

Christmas Stars

Craft-Stick "JOY" Star

by Linda Bloomgren

Make a quick ornament that costs just pennies!

Materials
- Five craft sticks
- One glitter chenille stem
- Yellow watercolor paint
- 9" of ¼" ribbon
- Thick craft glue
- Paintbrush, scissors

Instructions

1 Make the star. See photo. Glue craft sticks together to form star. Paint star yellow. Let dry.

2 Decorate the star. From chenille stem cut four lengths: 1¼", 1½", 2½", and 4". Bend 2" length into "J" and 4" length into "O". For "Y", bend ¼" of 1¼" length over center of 1½" piece. Glue letters on star.

3 Finish up. For hanger, thread ribbon through top of star and tie ends together. Cut ends at a slant.

Craft-Stick Whirling Star

by Sherry J. Bloom

Materials
- 70 craft sticks
- Wooden star shape
- 21" length of monofilament thread
- Metallic gold paint
- Gold glitter
- Brush-on gloss sealer*
- Thick craft glue
- Hammer and nail, paintbrushes, scissors

*Mod Podge® was used for this project.

Instructions

1 Paint the star. Use hammer and nail to make hole ⅜" down from one star point. Paint star gold. Sprinkle on glitter. Repeat on other side.

2 Make the craft stick sets. Place dab of glue in center of one craft stick. See Figure 1. Place second craft stick on a diagonal across first stick with centers crossing. Continue placing and gluing eight more sticks in the same way working in a clockwise direction. Make 4 more sets using 10 craft sticks for each set. Make 2 sets using 9 craft sticks each. Let the 7 sets dry.

Figure 1

3 Make the hanger and hang the star. See Figure 2. For hanger, cut 9" length of thread. Knot ends to form loop. Glue knot on center of one craft stick. Glue craft stick on *top* of one set of nine craft sticks with knot between sticks. Push remaining (12") thread through hole in star. Knot ends to form loop. Glue knot on remaining craft stick. Glue single craft stick on *bottom* of other set of nine craft sticks.

Figure 2

4 Build the spiral. Begin with set that has star. Glue each set of sticks on top of the other *ending with the hanger set.* Let glue dry between sets.

5 Finish up. For shiny, durable finish, brush 2-3 coats of sealer on craft sticks.

Make this delightful gift in just a few hours!

The Nativity & Epiphany
Clothespin Epiphany

by Blanche Lind

Many Nativity scenes depict the newborn Jesus in a manger with Shepherds, barn animals, and the Wise Men in attendance. However, the Bible makes it clear that the Wise Men did not arrive to visit Jesus until Jesus was some weeks old. The church calendar remembers the visitation of the Wise Men during Epiphany, not during the Christmas season.

Celebrate Christmas by making these adorable figures!

Bible Passage:
**Mathew
Chapter 2, Verses 1 - 12**

Materials

General
- One 2½ Kant-Roll Square miniature clothespin
- Acrylic paint: flesh and white
- One 1" diameter wooden heart
- Chenille stems: white, or to match color of robes
- Black fine-point permanent marker
- Trims: metallic cords, ribbons, or others
- Low temperature glue gun and glue sticks
- Flat paintbrush, old scissors or wire cutters, ruler, scissors

For Mary
- Paper twist: white and light blue
- Small amount of curly hair
- Miniature baby

For Joseph
- Paper twist: tan and dark blue
- Small amount of brown wavy hair
- Brown acrylic paint
- One craft pick

For Wisemen
- Metallic paper twist (colors of choice)
- Gifts: small gold beads or other jewelry findings

Instructions
Note: Adult supervision is needed when using a glue gun.

1 Basic instructions for all figures.
Paint body and base.
Paint clothespins flesh. Let dry. For base, paint one side and edges of heart white. Let dry. Turn base over and paint back. Let dry. For Mary's face, see Figure 1. Use marker to draw face onto wide portion of clothespin as shown. For Joseph and Wisemens' faces, see Figure 2. Use marker to draw faces onto wide portion of clothespins as shown. Let dry.

Figure 1

Figure 2

Add the arms and clothes. (For all figures except Joseph.) For inner robe, cut a piece of paper twist 1¾" in length. Untwist paper. Starting and ending at back, wrap paper twist around clothespin. Overlap ends and glue down. For arms, cut chenille stems into 2¾" lengths. Center arm section at back of body and glue into place. Shape arms by bending arms around to front of body.

For outer robe, cut a second robe from contrasting paper twist. Center and glue robe over top of arms on back of body. Make snips in top of robe at sides for arms. Slide arms through slits so that top of robe covers top of first robe. Secure front of outer robe to front of body, leaving front of inner robe uncovered by outer robe.

For headdress, cut a 3" length of paper twist and unfold. See Figure 3. Cut 3" length to a width of 2".

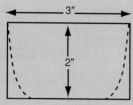

Figure 3

Round corners of paper twist as shown. Slightly fold straight edge of headdress under, then, center on front of head and glue down (folded edge on under side). Glue headdress to sides of head. Shape headdress over top of head to back of body. For headbands, wrap and glue gold braid or trim around top of head. Trim bottom of headdress if needed. **(Option:** Cut tiny crowns from metallic gold paper and glue to top of heads.)

2 Finish Up. For stands, glue bodies to heart bases so that point of heart is facing forward. To finish the Wisemen, bend arms so that ends of arms touch. For gifts, glue beads or other miniature jewelry findings in "hands."

To finish Joseph. To make outer robe, cut a three-inch length of paper twist. Untwist paper. Trim to a 2½" width. Fold paper twist in half widthwise. To fit the robe over arms, cut two slits in paper ¾" from each end and up to fold line. Fit and shape robe to figure by placing robe over arms. Glue wavy hair to to top and sides of head. Tie a 4" piece of metallic cord around top of head. Secure knot with glue, then trim ends of cord. For staff, cut craft stick to 2" length. Paint rounded end brown. Let dry. Glue staff to hand.

To finish Mary. Glue a small amount of curly hair to top of head at front. For swaddling clothes, cut a small piece of white paper twist to fit around baby. Glue cloth around baby. Glue baby into Mary's arms.

Starry-Night Nativity

by Janna Britton

Wooden stars form a frame around the manger.

Materials
- 4" diameter blue felt circle
- Two small angel charms*
- 25 wooden stars*: 12 small, 11 medium, 2 large
- Three wooden mini craft sticks
- 6" thin gold cord
- Gold metallic spray paint
- Clear acrylic sealer
- Thick craft glue
- Scissors, wire cutters

Brass Angel Charms: #6258, #6259 by Creative Beginnings/Woodsies™ stars by Forster® were used for this project.

Instructions
Note: *Adult supervision is needed when using wire cutters.*

1 Prepare the angels, stars, and sticks. Use wire cutters to remove loops from angel charms. Spray charms with sealer. Paint all stars gold.

Let dry. Use scissors to cut sticks for nativity as follows: two 1¼" lengths for roof, two 1" lengths for walls, two ½" lengths for manger bottom, four ¼" lengths for manger legs.

2 Make the frame. See photo. Glue a row of 9 medium and 2 large stars around outside of felt circle as desired. Glue three medium stars and eleven small stars on top of first row as desired.

3 Make the scene. See photo. For manger, arrange sticks as shown and glue in place. Glue one small star to top of manger roof. Glue angels facing star.

4 Finish up. For hanger, tie cord ends together to form loop. Glue knot to back of frame.

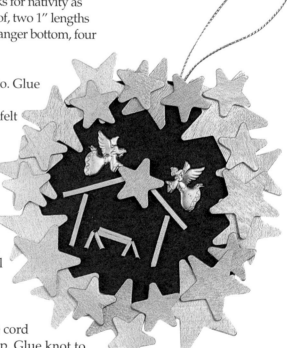

Pinecone Stable

by Janice Jones

Materials

- Two to three medium pinecones
- Miniature nativity figures
- 6" x 12" piece of heavy cardboard
- 2" x 2" piece of posterboard
- Shredded raffia or sawdust
- Three straight pins
- Gold paint
- Gold glitter
- Thick craft glue
- Paper, pencil, ruler, scissors, old scissors

Instructions

1 **Trace and cut out star pattern on this page.** Follow directions on pattern.

2 **Make the stable.** Cut cardboard into piece 1½" x 10". See Figure 1. Bend into an A-frame shape so the bottom measures 3" and the sides 3½". Glue top together. Insert pins to hold while glue dries. To make back, lay stable on cardboard and mark triangle shape. Cut out triangle. Run a line of glue all the way around stable and glue back in place. Place a book onto back to hold in place while it dries.

3½" **3½"**

3"

Figure 1

3 **Make the roof.** Trim cardboard if necessary. Cut pinecone petals (scales) with old scissors. For roof, glue a row of petals across bottom of one side with the thicker end down. Add a second row. Continue to add rows until you reach the peak. Repeat on other side of roof.

4 **Finish up.** Cut small pieces of petals. Glue petals all around opening for a finished look. Glue figures in place. Glue small amount of raffia or sawdust on floor. Glue glitter on star. Add star as shown in photo.

STAR
(cut 1 from posterboard)

Angels

A Choir of Foam-Plate Angels

by Linda Bloomgre

They're guaranteed to turn out heavenly!

Materials (for one angel)
- One 10" foam plate
- Chenille stem (for hair color of choice)
- Gold glitter stem
- Colored paper (for face color of choice)
- 8" of metallic thread
- Three adhesive stars
- Markers: red, black
- Rubber cement, scissors, plastic tape

It's almost a miracle how fast & easy these go together!

Instructions

1 Trace and cut out patterns on page 46. Follow directions on patterns.

2 Make the angel's body. Tape wings to back of body. Draw eyes and mouth on paper face with markers. Glue face on head.

3 Add the hair and halo. For hair, cut 7" piece from chenille stem. Shape stem to fit head. Roll free ends into curls as shown. Lay hair in place. For halo, cut 3" piece of glitter stem. Wrap glitter stem halo around hair and head. The halo will hold the hair in place.

4 Finish up. Add the 3 adhesive stars as shown. For hanger, tape ends of metallic thread to back of wings.

Option: For colorful angels, cut patterns from colored foam meat or vegetable trays.

Wallpaper Angel

by Doris M. Schmidt

Materials
- Wallpaper scraps
- One 1" wooden doll head
- 12" of ¼" satin ribbon: choice of color
- One small satin ribbon rose: choice of color
- One metallic silver chenille stem
- Spaghnum moss
- Low-temp glue gun and glue sticks
- Paper, pencil, ruler, scissors

She's so quick and easy—make several!

Instructions

Note: Adult supervision is needed when using a glue gun.

1 Trace and cut out patterns on page 45. Follow directions on patterns.

2 Make the angel. Glue wrong sides of wings together. Fold gown and 2 sleeves into cone shapes. Glue to hold. Fold top of gown over ¼" and glue down. Glue flat side of doll head on top of gown. See illustration. Glue sleeves on sides of gown. Wrap ribbon around neck. Make a bow. Cut ribbon ends at a slant. Glue rose on bow knot. Glue wings on back of gown.

3 Finish up. For hair, glue moss on top of head. For halo, cut a 4" long chenille stem. Form circle and twist ends to secure. Glue halo on hair.

Lacy Spoon-Angel

by Dale-Marie Bryan

Bible Passage:
Psalm
Chapter 91, Verses 11-12

Materials
• Plastic, silver, or silver-plate teaspoon
• 6" length of 4" white pre-gathered lace
• 12" length of ⅛" white ribbon
• 12" metallic chenille stem
• 6" x 21" piece of white or pink netting or tulle
• 12" length of silver metallic thread
• Black fine-line permanent marker
• Red acrylic paint (optional)
• Jewelry glue
• Low-temp glue gun and sticks
• Scissors, ruler, cotton swab, white thread and needle, paper towels

Recycle a garage-sale or picnic spoon!

Instructions
Note: Adult supervision is needed when using a glue gun and sticks.

1 **Make the face.** Use marker to draw features on inside bowl of spoon. For cheeks, dip one end of swab in red paint. Blot swab on paper towel to remove excess paint. Dab cheeks on face. Let dry.

2 **Make the hanger**. Fold metallic thread in half. Knot thread together near cut ends. Slip this thread loop over spoon. Position and knot under bowl of spoon. Use jewelry glue to secure knot on back of spoon. Let dry.

3 **Begin the dress.** Fold lace in half, right sides together and unfinished edges even. Thread needle with white thread and knot. Sew edges together with a running stitch ¼" from the unfinished edges to make a tube. Knot and cut thread.

4 **Finish the dress.** Thread the needle again and knot. With lace tube still inside out, sew a running stitch along one bound edge of lace to gather it. Leaving thread and needle in place, slip handle of spoon into tube, so lace covers face, gathered edge is at neck of spoon, and spoon handle is visible. Pull thread around neck and knot in place. Cut away needle and excess thread. Turn dress right side out so it covers spoon handle and face is showing. Center seam at back of spoon and glue in place.

5 **Make the halo.** Cut 3" length from chenille stem. Twist ends together to make circle. Use jewelry glue to glue halo in place.

6 **Finish up.** To make wings, tie tulle into a bow with 4"-5" tails. Use glue gun and sticks to glue bow on back of angel's neck. Tie ⅛" ribbon in a bow. Glue bow on front of dress.

Palm Sunday

Newspaper Palm Tree

by Frank Zemaitis

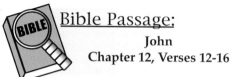

Bible Passage:
John
Chapter 12, Verses 12-16

On the day we now celebrate as Palm Sunday, Jesus fulfilled the prophecy that the Lord would arrive upon a lowly animal. As Jesus rode through the streets of Jerusalem on a donkey the people put garments and palm branches in the road. Follow these simple step-by-step directions to make your own palm tree. If you like you can use water colors or tempura paints to paint the newspapers before rolling and tearing them. Be sure to use a very thin layer of paint and dry the newspapers thoroughly before making your tree.

Roll a full sheet of newspaper halfway. The ends should be about one and a half inches wide.

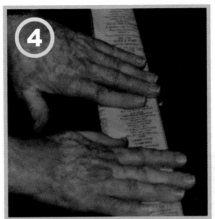
Add a second sheet and roll about halfway. Then repeat with a third and fourth.

Place one piece of tape in the middle.

Flatten one third of the end.

Tear a third of the way down. If it is too hard, an adult can help.

Flatten again between the tears.

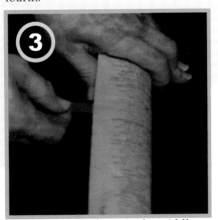
Tear again between the first tears.

Shake the loose end and find the center.

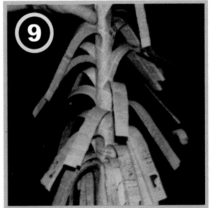
With a jerky motion gently pull up the center coils. Keep pulling until it stops.

Easter

Christ is risen!

Butterfly Easter Plaque

by Linda Bloomgren

Brighten your classroom for just pennies!

Christ is risen!

Materials
- 9" white paper plate
- 2" x 7" white paper strip
- 6" square poster board
- One craft stick
- 18" length of yarn
- Markers
- Thick craft glue
- Transparent tape
- Paper, pencil, scissors

Instructions

1 Trace and cut out patterns on page 47. Follow directions on patterns. Use butterfly pattern to trace butterfly on center of paper plate.

2 Decorate the butterfly. For body, use marker to color craft stick black. See photo. Glue the stick on center of butterfly. Use black marker to draw antennae. Color wings and decorate plate as desired.

3 Finish up. Glue words under butterfly as shown. Use tape to attach yarn hanger on back of plate.

Option: An older child or adult can make a 3-D butterfly by cutting around the wings with a craft knife. After cutting, gently push wings forward. **Note:** *Adult supervision is needed when using a craft knife.*

Pom-Pom Easter Chicks

by Karen Taylor

Made in minutes with just a few craft supplies!

Materials (for one chick)
- Two yellow pom-poms: 1", 1½"
- Felt scraps: orange, yellow
- Two 8mm wiggle eyes
- Thick craft glue
- Paper, pencil, scissors

Instructions

1 Trace and cut out patterns on page 46. Follow directions on patterns.

2 Make the chicks. Glue 1" pom-pom on top of 1½" pom-pom. See photo. Glue on wiggle eyes. For beak, fold on line. Glue beak on face. See Figure 1. Glue feathers on one wing as shown. Reverse for second wing. Glue one wing on each side of body.

3 Finish up. Glue knot on tie. Glue tie and feet on body.

feather

Wing

feather

Figure 1

Folded-Paper Baskets by Monica Graham

Paper and glue — that's all it takes!

Bible Passage:
John
Chapter 20, Verses 1-18

Materials	
•Construction paper: one 9" x 12" sheet and scrap	•Jelly beans or small candy
•Craft glue	•Clothespins
•Cellophane grass	•Pencil
	•Ruler
	•Scissors

Instructions

1 Shape the basket. Measure and cut one piece of paper into a 9" square. For handle, cut a 1" wide x 9" long strip. To make guide-line folds, see Figures 1 and 2. Fold paper in half diagonally, opposite corners together and press fold. Unfold paper. Make second fold in the same way matching opposite corners. Open paper. See Figure 3. Fold corners to center of paper and press down folds. Turn paper over. See Figure 4. Fold all four corners to center and press down folds. Turn paper over. See Figure 5. Fold center points to outside edges and press down folds. Turn paper over. See Figure 6. Fold center points to outside edges and press down folds. Press down all folds, creasing paper with thumb.

2 Open the basket. (*Note: Basket will not look exactly like finished basket when first opened. Basket bottom will need additional shaping and it will need to be glued together to hold its proper shape.*) See Figure 7. Turn paper over. Insert index fingers over and inside of flaps A and B. Place thumbs at C and D. Place middle fingers on side opposite C and D. Gently pull away from center of basket. Remove index fingers and squeeze basket together. To square and crease bottom, push sides towards center while pressing down on table. Open flaps E and F in the same way.

3 Finish Up. See Figure 8. The figure shows what the finished basket should look like.(*Note: You may not get it right the first time — but keep trying!*) Glue side flaps together. Glue side flaps to sides of basket. Glue ends of handle to opposite sides of basket on inside. Hold flaps and handle in place with clothespins until dry. Fill with grass, jelly beans, or candy.

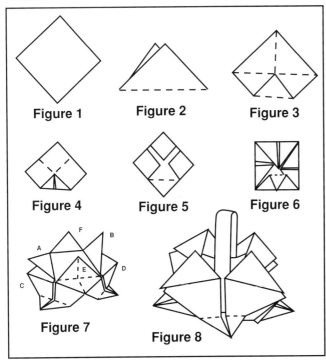

Figure 1   Figure 2   Figure 3

Figure 4   Figure 5   Figure 6

Figure 7   Figure 8

Easter Crosses

Ribbon Cross Bookmarks

by Jan Koepsell

Recycled greeting cards make colorful backgrounds!

Materials
- Recycled greeting cards
- ½" or ⅝" ribbon
- Paper, pencil, craft knife, scissors, ruler

Instructions
Note: Adult supervision is needed when using a craft knife

1 Make Cross. See Figure 1. From greeting card, cut a cross shape that measures 3" x 4½". Use craft knife to cut ¾" slits as indicated.

2 Weave ribbon. For each cross, cut one 6" and one 8" ribbon length. See Figure 1. Thread 8" ribbon through the four horizontal slits. Center ribbon. Repeat for 6" ribbon, threading through two vertical slits. Cut ribbon ends at a slant.

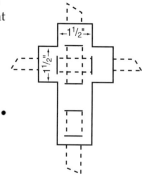

Group Tip: *Make several cardboard crosses. Children can trace these onto their greeting cards.*

Bottle-Cap Cross*

by Kathy Cisneros

Bible Passage:
1 Corithians Chapter 1, Verse 18

Materials
- Six two-liter plastic bottle caps
- Acrylic paint: color of choice
- Trims: string beads, ribbon, metallic cord, beads, miniature silk flowers, or other
- Crystal glitter
- Six small pictures (religious or other)
- Thick craft glue or low temperature glue gun and sticks
- Cotton swabs, paintbrush, pencil, scissors

Reprinted with permission from "Recreational Recycling" by Kathy Cisneros.

Instructions
Note: *Adult supervision is needed when using a glue gun.*

1 Wash and dry caps. To cut pictures, use a cap as a pattern. Center picture under cap. Trace around cap onto picture. Cut out picture. Set aside.

2 See Photo. Glue caps together as shown. (**Note**: If not using a glue gun, let glue dry between steps.)

3 Turn cross over, opening side down and paint backs and sides of cross. Let dry.

4 Use cotton swab to spread glue on inside of caps. Fill each cap with glitter. Let dry. Shake out excess glitter. Glue pictures into each cap.

5 Wrap and glue trims around outside edges of cross. Glue beads or flowers to top.

6 To hang, fold a length of cord in half and knot ends forming a loop. Glue loop by knot to top of cross.

Glue-Stick Cross

by Janna Britton

Materials

- Six oval glitter glue sticks*: two blue and four silver
- 36 inches of silver cord
- 15 sparkle pony beads: 12 regular silver, one silver heart, and two blue hearts
- Low-temperature glue gun*
- Ruler, scissors

*Stick-a-Roo low temperature glue gun and Crafty Magic Melt oval glue sticks from Adhesive Technologies were used for this project.)

Instructions

1 Heat glue gun with silver glue stick. Measure and cut one blue stick in half.

2 See Photo. For cross, glue halves to sides of whole blue stick as shown.

3 Let dry. For trim, work from the back of cross. Squeeze glue into loops and squiggles so glue drapes down at least ¼" over sides.

4 For hanger loop, make a glue loop large enough for two lengths of cord to fit through at top of cross. Reinforce loop with several layers of glue. Let cool. Glue on silver heart.

5 To make the necklace, fold cord in half. Thread center of cord through hanger. Bring ends of cord through loop in cord and pull knot closed. String beads on each side of cord in the following order: three silver, one heart, then three more silver. Knot ends of cord together.

Lenten Banner Cross

by Terri Quillen

Materials

- 1" round wooden doll pin stand
- 1" circle of felt or cardboard
- One jumbo craft stick*
- Two regular craft sticks*
- Two purple fabric strips: 1½" x 7" and 3" x 8"
- One bunch lavender artificial flowers on a wire stem
- Low-temp glue gun, heavy-duty scissors, thread, ruler

*Craft sticks by Forster®, Inc. were used in this project.

Instructions

Note: *Adult supervision is needed when using a glue gun and when cutting craft sticks.*

1 **Begin banner.** See photo. For swag, use fingers to gather one short end of 3" x 8" fabric. Wrap and knot thread around gathers. Cut thread ends.

Repeat on other end of fabric. Glue gathered ends of fabric on opposite ends of one regular craft stick.

2 **Make support beam.** Glue felt or cardboard circle on bottom of doll pin stand. See Figure 1. Use scissors to cut a blunt

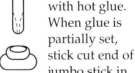

Figure 1

point on one end of jumbo craft stick. Fill doll stand hole with hot glue. When glue is partially set, stick cut end of jumbo stick in glue and hold in place until glue sets. For added strength, add a little more glue where stick and stand meet.

3 **Make crossbeam.** See photo. Glue swaged craft stick horizontally on front of jumbo stick, ¾" from top. Glue second regular craft stick on back of jumbo stick, sandwiching gathered ends of fabric between the ends of the two horizontal sticks.

4 **Finish banner.** Fold remaining fabric strip in thirds lengthwise. See photo. Fold fabric in half over one end of crossbeam. Glue in place. Wrap stemmed flowers around bottom of cross.

Tissue-Paper Tongues of Fire

by Georgianne Detzner

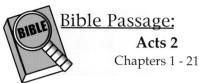

Bible Passage:

Acts 2
Chapters 1 - 21

Materials
- 12" foam wreath
- Red, yellow, and orange tissue paper
- Yellow and red construction paper
- 12" white chenille stems
- Black marker
- Scissors, hole punch, pencil, paper, ruler

Instructions

1 **Trace and cut out pattern on page 46.** Follow directions on pattern. Punch holes in tongue as shown on pattern. See photo. Write *LOVE* in language of choice on tongue. *Note: Research your own language preference or see chart accompanying this article.* Thread chenille stem through holes on yellow paper tongue so 1" sticks up from top.

2 **Make the flames.** For each tongue of fire cut four 7" squares of tissue paper: one yellow, one orange, and two red. Stack tissue paper squares on top of one another alternating colors. Use pencil point to poke a hole through center of all four layers.

3 **Attach flames to tongue.** Thread tissue flames onto stem and fold up around yellow tongue. Wrap stem around bottom of flames two times leaving several inches of stem. Cut stem remaining on bottom of flame so ½" is left for inserting flame into wreath.

4 **Make the centerpiece.** To cover sides of wreath, cut four 2" x 10½" lengths of yellow construction paper. Glue lengths together overlapping ½" to make a 2" x 40½" length. Write *Every man heard them speak in his own tongue. — ACTS 2* on paper strip. Glue paper strip around wreath. Stick flames into wreath.

In ACTS 2 we hear the story of the Holy Spirit's ascent upon the disciples in the form of tongues of fire and the miracle that occurred when people from many lands heard the word of God in their own language! Encourage your students to translate God's primary message — the message of LOVE — into another language and make symbolic tissue-paper tongues of fire. As each child puts his or her flame into the centerpiece, they are reminded of the unifying power of LOVE.

Some Languages of Love:

Ahava (Hebrew)
Mitosc (Polish)
Aime (French)
Prem (Hindi)
Amore (Italian)
Sa rang (Korean)
Liebe (German)
Upendo (Swahili)
Mahal (Filipino)

(Chinese)

Любовь (Russian)

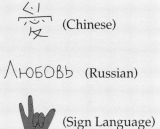 (Sign Language)

Mother's Father's Day Pop-Bottle Flower Frame

by Janna Britton

Materials

- Pink and green craft foam
- Parchment paper
- Thick cardboard
- Three 20oz. plastic soda bottles
- Plaster-of-paris
- Yellow acrylic paint
- Green paint marker
- Tangerine glitter fabric paint
- Low-temp glue gun
- Scissors, ruler, pencil

Instructions

Note: Adult supervision is needed when using a glue gun.

Figure 1

1 Make the flowers. See Figure 1. Cut a 1½" tall section from bottom of each bottle. Recycle tops of bottles. Following manufacturer's directions, pour plaster-of-paris into bottle bottoms to level of about ½". Let set and dry overnight. Unmold flowers.

2 Paint the flowers. Use yellow to paint flowers. Let dry. Use tangerine to paint centers of flowers. Let dry overnight.

3 Trace and cut out pattern on page 46. Follow directions on pattern. Use paint marker to draw veins on leaves.

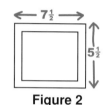

Figure 2

4 Make the frame. Cut one 5½" x 7½" rectangle each from pink foam, parchment paper, and cardboard. See Figure 2. To make frame opening, measure and lightly mark a 1" border around foam rectangle. Cut out center of frame.

5 Finish up. Write Bible verse in center of parchment paper. Sandwich Bible verse paper between frame and cardboard backing. Glue in place. Glue flowers on frame. Let dry.

Shoe-Polish Desk Set

by Mabel Martin

Materials

- Containers of choice (boxes with lids, cans or others)
- Masking tape
- Brown liquid shoe polish
- Gold braid or other trim
- Thick craft glue
- Scissors

Instructions

1 To cover containers, tear off ½" to 1" lengths of masking tape. Starting at the bottom of the container and working up, press tape onto container. Continue adding tape, overlapping edges slightly and positioning the tape at different angles.

2 To finish, paint covered container with shoe polish. Let dry. Glue trim around container as desired. Let dry.

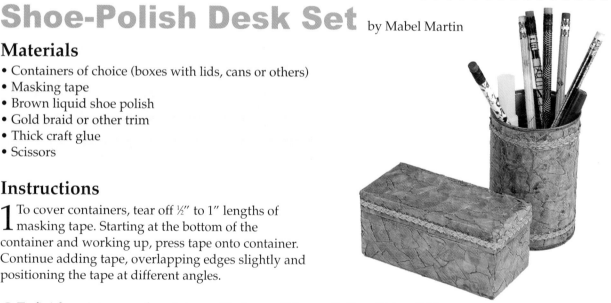

Option: Write a Bible verse or appropriate quote such as "The Pen is Mightier than the Sword" on paper and glue it on top of box or around pencil can.

Vacation Bible School

Prayer Journals

by Terri Quillen

Bible Passage:
**1 Thessalonians
Chapter 5, Verses 16-18**

Materials
- One 9" x 12" piece of stiffened felt*
- Four pieces of 8½" x 11" typing or computer paper
- 16" of thick craft or rug yarn
- Gold metallic paint-marker pen
- Low-temp glue gun and sticks, pinking shears, ruler, hole punch, pencil

Stiffened EAZY FELT from Consumer Products Enterprises, Inc. was used for this project. For more information see "Where to Find It" on page 48.

Use a simple book-making technique and then decorate your journal with beads, seeds, beans, buttons, or ribbon.

Instructions
Note: *Adult supervision is needed when using a glue gun and sticks.*

1 Begin the journal. For covers, use pinking shears to cut two 6" x 9" pieces of felt. For pages, stack papers and fold them in half to measure 5½" x 8½". Use pinking shears to cut papers around all four sides making eight 5½" x 8½" pages.

2 Make the holes. See Figure 1. For front cover, measure and punch holes on one piece of felt as shown. For back cover, place front cover on top of second piece of felt with sides lined up evenly. Use pencil to mark hole positions. Use

Figure 1

hole punch to make holes on back cover. Mark holes on stack of pages in the same way using holes on the front or back cover as a guide. Punch the marked holes.

3 Make the journal. Cut yarn into two 8" lengths. Sandwich pages between book covers so holes line up. See journal sketch. Thread yarn pieces through holes and tie as shown. Cut off excess yarn ends.

4 Decorate the journal. Use paint marker to write *Seeds of Faith* on front cover. Glue on buttons, beads, beans, ribbon, or seeds as desired.

Paper Roll Angel Tree Topper

by Helen Rafson

Materials

- Toilet-paper roll
- 2" x 2½" foam egg
- Yellow curly doll hair*
- Two 4 mm black beads
- Two ½" white buttons
- 7½ " of metallic gold rickrack
- 6" length of ⅝" white lace
- Nylon stocking scrap
- Felt scraps: pink, white
- White acrylic paint
- Clear glitter paint*
- Brush-on blush make-up
- Thick craft glue
- Paintbrush, paper, pencil, ruler, scissors, cotton swab, heavy thread

*Heavy Metals Clear Liquid Glitter Paint Glimmer by Deco Art and doll hair by Darice, Inc. were used for this project.

Instructions

1 **Trace and cut out patterns on page 41.** Follow directions on patterns. Cut ½ " off one end of toilet paper roll.

2 **For body, paint toilet paper roll with two coats of white paint.** Let dry. Paint roll and front of wings with two coats of glitter paint. Let dry.

3 **Fold each sleeve as indicated on pattern.** Glue each sleeve together along seam lines. See photo. Glue hands onto inside of sleeves, thumbs facing forward. Let dry. Glue sleeves onto sides of body.

4 **For face, fit stocking tightly over foam egg.** Bring excess stocking to pointed end of egg. Twist stocking several times. Tie and knot thread around excess stocking. Cut away excess thread and stocking.

5 **Glue on hair and bead eyes.** Let dry. Glue head onto body. For cheeks, use swab to brush on make-up. For collar, glue lace around neck. For halo, glue rickrack into a circle. See photo. Glue on halo and buttons as shown. Let dry.

Options:

Make angel with your hair, skin, and eye colors. Use your favorite colors of construction paper and paint instead of white. Make hair from curling ribbon, strips of crimped packing paper, or yarn. Substitute a chenille stem for her rickrack halo.

5 x 5 Tiny Angels

by Charlene Messerle

*Five little ones - -
each made from little
wooden hearts!*

Bible Passage:

**Psalm 148
Verses 1-2**

Materials

• Pre-cut wooden
hearts *: ten ⅞", fifteen
1⅛ "
• Five ½" wooden
beads
• Curly doll hair*:
auburn, brown, blond
• Acrylic paint: blue,
green, red, yellow,
purple, black, metallic
gold
• Five 1½ " lengths of
small primary-colored,
pre-strung beads
• Thick craft glue
• Glue gun and sticks,
paintbrush, scissors,
monofilament thread
* Mini-Curl Curly Hair by
One & Only Creations ®
and Forster® Woodsies™
wooden hearts were used for
this project.   .

Instructions

1 **Paint the wood pieces.**
For each angel's skirt,
paint three large hearts a
primary color. For wings,
paint all small hearts
gold. Let dry. See photo.
Use tip of brush to apply
polka dots in a
contrasting color on each
skirt heart and facial
features on each bead. Let
dry.

2 **Make the angels.** See
photo. To form skirts,
glue each set of three
large hearts into a
pyramid shape, heart
points up. Glue head
beads on top of skirts.

3 **Make the hangers.** Cut
thread into five 5"
lengths. Tie the two ends
of each length in a knot.
Cut ends close to knot.
Glue a knot on top of each
angel head.

4 **Finish up.** See photo.
Glue on hair and bead
necklaces. For wings, glue
two gold hearts, points
touching, on back of each
angel. Let dry.

Wooden Angel Ornament

by Angie Wilhite

Materials

• Two ⅞" wide precut wooden
hearts*
• ¾" diameter precut wooden circle*
• 1¼" diameter precut wooden circle*
• Scraps of red, gold, and antique white felt
• 10" length of ⅛" red satin ribbon
• Two 6mm wiggle eyes
• 6" square of instant double stick adhesive*
• Red fine-line permanent marker
• Glue gun and glue sticks (optional)
• Thick craft glue
• Pencil, scissors, cotton swab, pink blush
*Woodsies™ wooden shapes from Forster®, Inc. and Coats Instant
Stick-n-Hold® from Coats and Clark were used for this project.*

Instructions

1 **Get started.** Following manufacturer's directions,
apply double stick adhesive on back of felt scraps.

2 **Make the wings.** Use wooden heart to trace and cut
two hearts from gold felt. Remove paper backing
and press felt shapes on wooden shapes.

3 **Make the face.** Use ¾" wooden circle to trace and
cut a circle from antique white felt. Remove paper
backing and press felt on wooden shape.

4 **Make the body.** Use 1¼" wooden circle to trace and
cut a circle from red felt. Remove paper backing and
press felt on wooden shape.

5 **Assemble the angel.** See photo. Glue face on top of
body. Glue wings on back of head. Glue eyes on
face. For cheeks, use cotton swab to apply blush on
face. Use marker to dot mouth on face.

6 **Make the bow and hanging loop.** For bow, cut a 4"
length from ribbon. Tie ribbon into a bow. Cut
ribbon ends at a slant. Glue bow on face. For hanging
loop, glue remaining ribbon ends together on back of
head.

Bible-Verse Wreath

by Susan Payne

Each piece of paper hides a Bible verse!

Express yourself by picking five favorite paper colors!

Materials
- One 12" square of black poster board
- Five 6" x 11" pieces of colored construction paper
- One 3½" and one 8½" circle for tracing (salad plate and jar lid work well)
- White school glue
- Ruler, pencil, scissors

Instructions

1 **Cut paper rectangles.** See Figure 1. Use pencil and ruler to mark thirty-three 1" x 2" rectangles on each piece of paper as shown. Cut out rectangles. Write a Bible verse on each paper.

2 **Fold the paper triangles.** See Figure 2. To find the middle of each rectangle, fold in half as shown. Unfold. See Figure 3. Fold over top two corners of each rectangle to form triangles as shown.

3 **Make the circle guides for placing triangles.** Center and trace large circle (plate) on black poster board. Center and trace small circle (jar lid) inside the large circle.

4 **Make the design.** Place top point of one triangle somewhere along small circle draw on poster board. Glue triangle in place so top point and bottom edge are not glued down. See photo. To place second triangle, slip bottom of triangle over point of first triangle. Glue back of second triangle onto poster board background. Continue adding triangles, alternating colors, until both circles are complete.

Suggestions for use:
- *After the wreath has been displayed for awhile, take it down and let each class member select one or more papers to read aloud to the class. Perhaps the person who originally wrote the verse would like to explain their choice.*

- *Have each member of the class select a paper color and a Bible verse. Have the students write part of their verse on each paper. When the wreath is assembled the students will know where their verse is "hidden" in the wreath.*

- *Make a "progressive" wreath by having children add folded papers as they memorize verses. When the wreath is completed celebrate their knowledge of the Bible!*

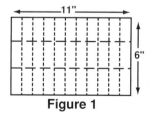

Figure 1

11"

6"

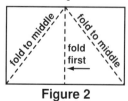

Figure 2

fold to middle

fold to middle

fold first

Figure 3

Wooden-Spoon Fish Necklace

by Janna Britton

Our designer sent the following story about the fish symbol!

"I was told that when believers in Jesus first met a new person, they would use their walking stick to draw a picture of a fish in the dirt. If the other person filled in the name of Jesus, a believer would know the newcomer was a believer, too, and could talk about Jesus."

Materials

- Wooden craft spoon
- White acrylic paint
- 12 pony beads: 2 each of six colors
- 30" of white nylon cord
- One 7mm jump ring
- Blue fine-point permanent marker
- Drill with ⅟₁₆" bit, paintbrush, needle-nose pliers, scissors

Instructions

Note: Adult supervision is needed when drilling holes.

1 Make the fish. See drawing. Use scissors to cut fish tail as shown. Paint fish white. Let dry. On front end of fish, drill hole for ring. Use blue marker to outline fish and write Jesus' name.

Note: Older children may want to write Jesus' name in Greek as shown.

2 Make the necklace. Use pliers to open jump ring. Slip ring through hole in fish. Use pliers to close ring. Thread cord through ring. String six beads on cord on each side of ring. Knot cord ends together.

Option: To make a magnet or pin, simply attach a magnet strip or glue a pin back on back of fish.

Holy Bible

by Jennifer Hearon

Make this clever keepsake for your favorite Bible scholar!

Materials

- 5-ounce bar of soap
- Construction paper: black, yellow
- Thick craft glue
- Black marker, black pen, ruler, scissors

Instructions

1 Prepare the paper. Cut one 1" x 11" strip and one 1½" x 2" piece from yellow paper. Cut one 4½" x 6" piece from black paper. Using black pen and ruler draw lines ⅛" apart along the **length** of yellow paper. Using marker, print the words "HOLY BIBLE" on the yellow paper rectangle.

2 Put the Bible together. See photo. Glue the yellow strip around edges of soap. For Bible cover, glue black paper around soap as shown. Glue yellow rectangle to front of bible.

The Sower of Seeds

by Sharon Clay

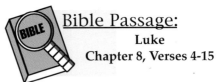

Bible Passage:
Luke
Chapter 8, Verses 4-15

Materials (For each)
- One miniature clay pot (2½" tall)
- Tempera paints (colors of choice)
- Cotton swabs
- One packet of seeds
- ¼" wide ribbon
- One copy of story
- Paper plates, newspapers

Instructions

1 Cover work area with newspapers. Pour a small amount of tempera paints onto separate paper plates. Using cotton swabs as paintbrushes, have the children decorate their pots while the story is read to them.

2 When pots are finished and dry, give each child a packet of seeds and a copy of the story that has been rolled and tied with ribbon. Tell the children how to plant and water their seeds.

The Sower and the Seed

A 🧑‍🌾 went out 2 🌱 some 🌰. As

he 🌱d the 🌰 5 🌰's Fell along the

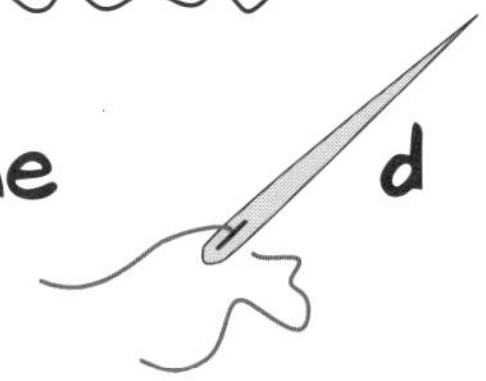

hard 🛤 and the 🐦🐦 came and

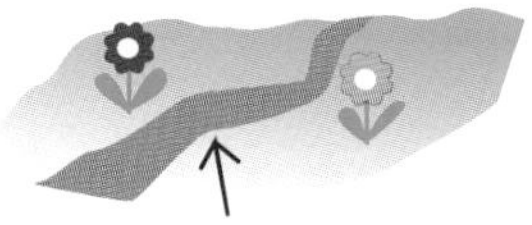

8 the 🌰 5 🌰s fell on shallow, 🪨y

ground. They quickly sprouted and grew into

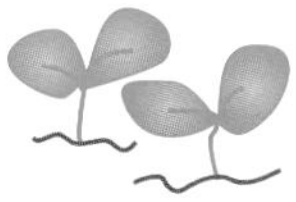

🌱. But w 🐓 the hot ☀ shone, the

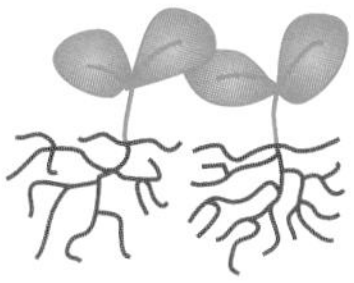

🌱 did 🪱 have 🥛, food, and protection of

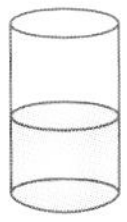

deep soil, 🌱 the 🌱 dried up and died.

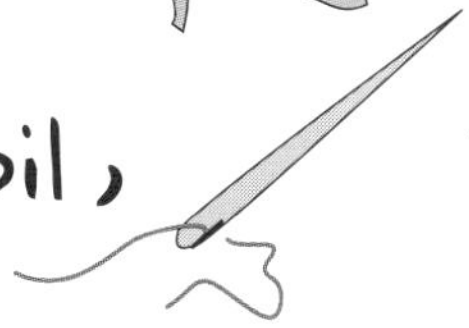

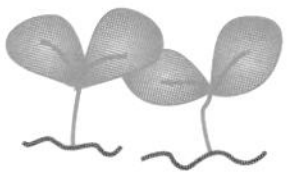

5 🌰s fell among 🌿. The 🌿 grew up and

choked out the good 🌱. But other 🌰 fell on

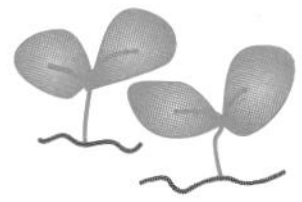

good ground and grew up into strong, healthy

🌱 Their roots went deep into the rich moist

soil and made a large crop of gr🌧. Mark 4:1-9

Burnt-Match Cross

by Helen V. Groves

Materials
- 120 burnt wooden kitchen matches
- Thick cardboard or thin plywood
- Thick craft glue
- Decoupage
- Paper, pencil, ruler, scissors

Instructions

Note: Adult supervision is needed when lighting matches.

1 **Cut a cross from cardboard or plywood.** See Figure 1 for size. Draw a line in the center of cross in both directions.

2 **Make the cross.** See Figure 2. Cut four ¾" match pieces (without burnt ends) and glue onto lines at center. Glue the four, 9-match sections. Glue the remaining sections with the number of matches shown.

Some Tips . . .
- Light matches one at a time and blow out immediately.
- Carefully wipe off burnt ends with tissue.
- Decoupage or varnish finished project.
- Glue picture hanger on back for displaying.
- Adapt size of pattern to make little cross with small wooden matches.

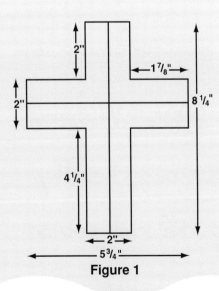

Figure 1

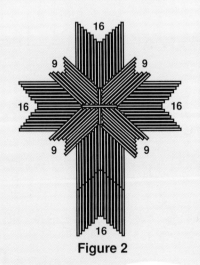

Figure 2

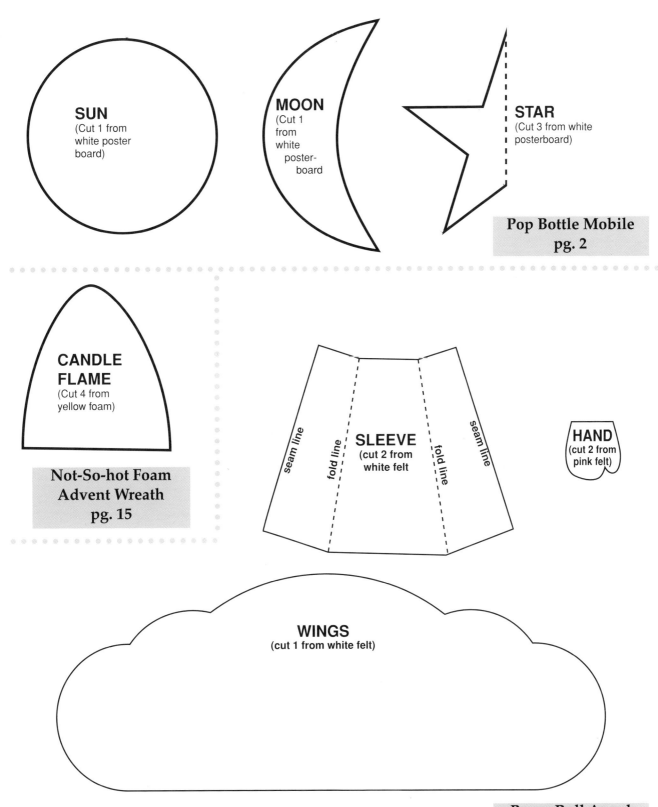

SUN
(Cut 1 from
white poster
board)

MOON
(Cut 1
from
white
poster-
board

STAR
(Cut 3 from white
posterboard)

Pop Bottle Mobile
pg. 2

**CANDLE
FLAME**
(Cut 4 from
yellow foam)

Not-So-hot Foam
Advent Wreath
pg. 15

seam line

fold line

SLEEVE
(cut 2 from
white felt)

fold line

seam line

HAND
(cut 2 from
pink felt)

WINGS
(cut 1 from white felt)

Paper-Roll Angel
Tree Topper
pg. 34

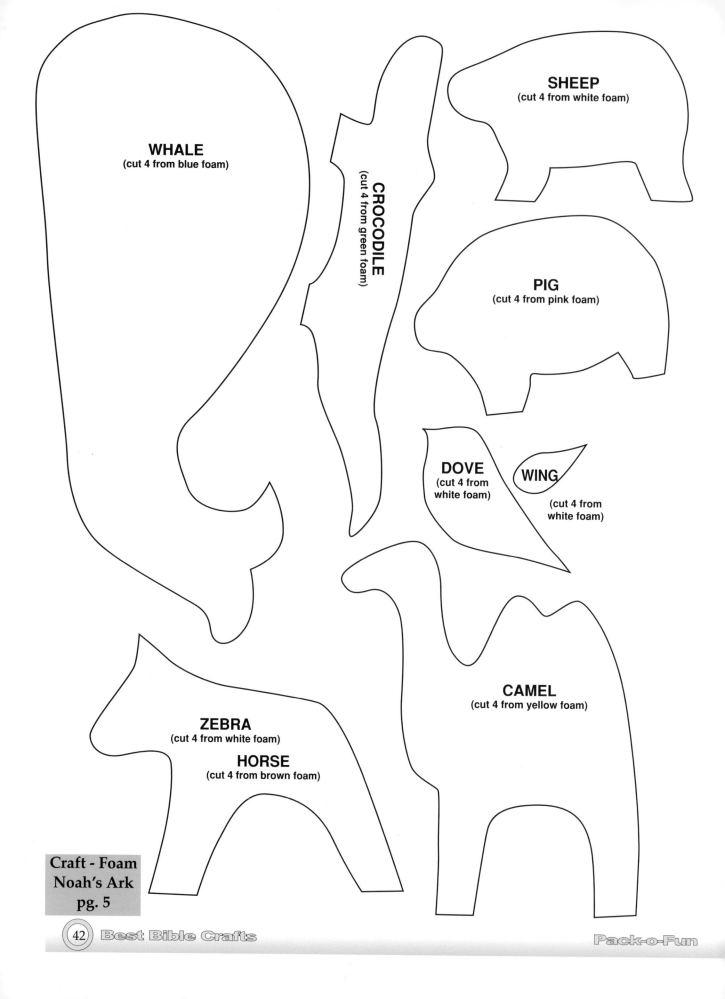

WHALE
(cut 4 from blue foam)

SHEEP
(cut 4 from white foam)

CROCODILE
(cut 4 from green foam)

PIG
(cut 4 from pink foam)

DOVE
(cut 4 from
white foam)

WING
(cut 4 from
white foam)

CAMEL
(cut 4 from yellow foam)

ZEBRA
(cut 4 from white foam)

HORSE
(cut 4 from brown foam)

Craft - Foam
Noah's Ark
pg. 5

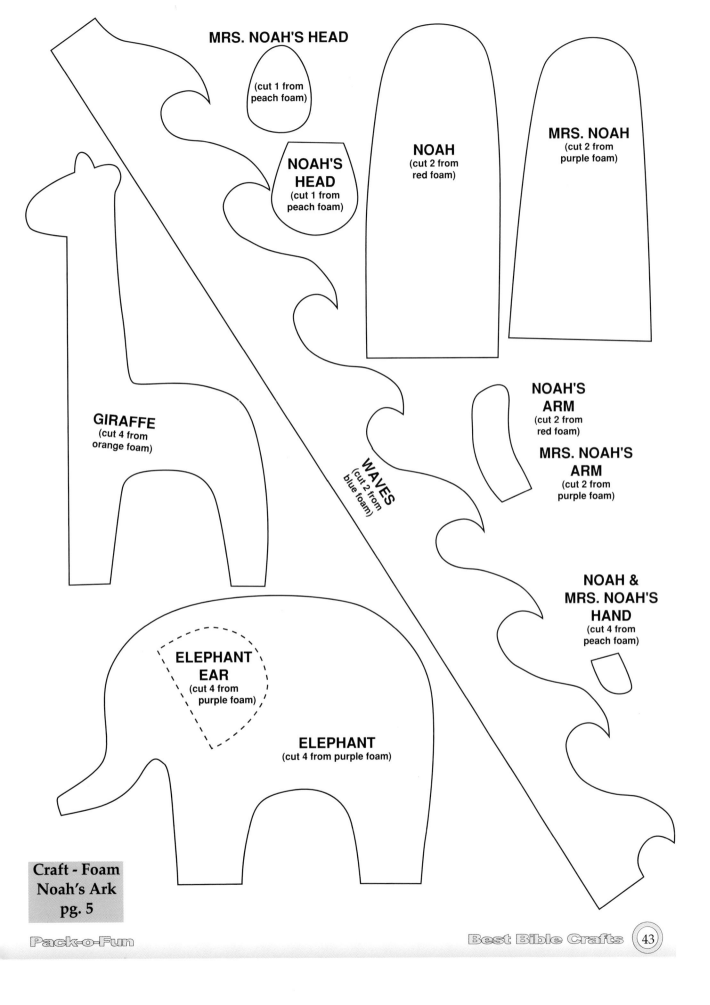

MRS. NOAH'S HEAD

(cut 1 from peach foam)

NOAH'S HEAD
(cut 1 from peach foam)

NOAH
(cut 2 from red foam)

MRS. NOAH
(cut 2 from purple foam)

GIRAFFE
(cut 4 from orange foam)

WAVES
(cut 2 from blue foam)

NOAH'S ARM
(cut 2 from red foam)

MRS. NOAH'S ARM
(cut 2 from purple foam)

NOAH & MRS. NOAH'S HAND
(cut 4 from peach foam)

ELEPHANT EAR
(cut 4 from purple foam)

ELEPHANT
(cut 4 from purple foam)

Craft - Foam Noah's Ark pg. 5

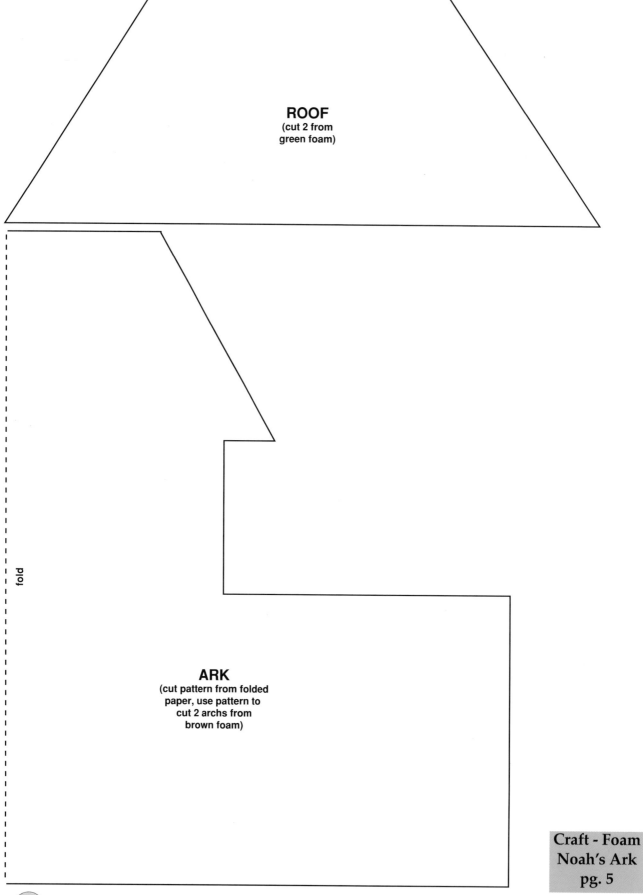

ROOF
(cut 2 from
green foam)

fold

ARK
(cut pattern from folded
paper, use pattern to
cut 2 archs from
brown foam)

Craft - Foam
Noah's Ark
pg. 5

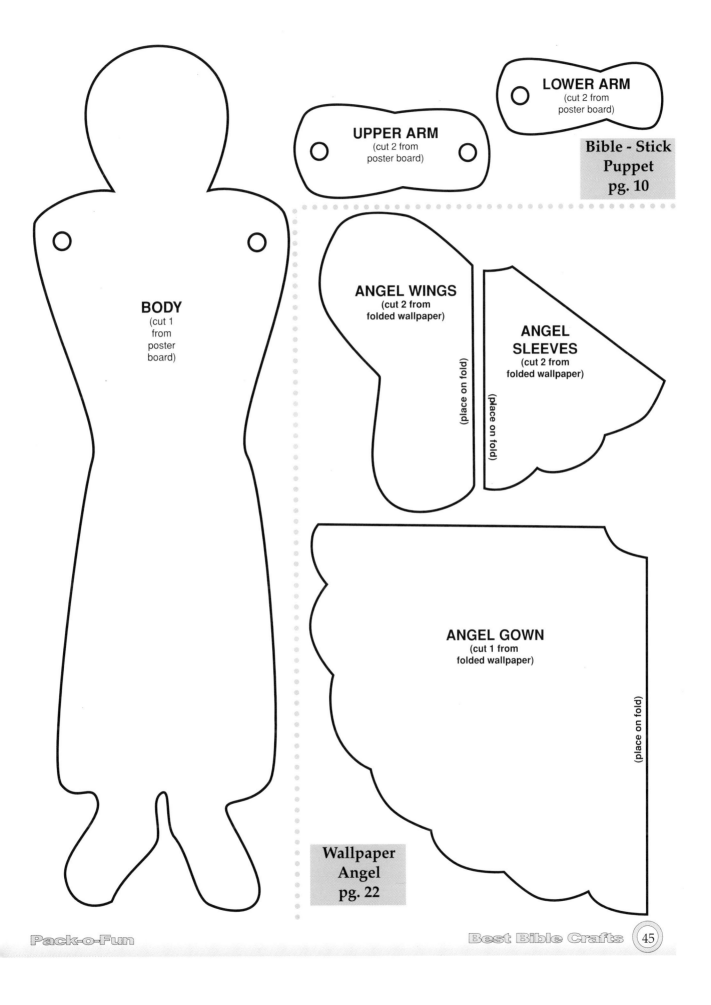

LOWER ARM
(cut 2 from
poster board)

UPPER ARM
(cut 2 from
poster board)

**Bible - Stick
Puppet
pg. 10**

BODY
(cut 1
from
poster
board)

ANGEL WINGS
(cut 2 from
folded wallpaper)

(place on fold)

ANGEL
SLEEVES
(cut 2 from
folded wallpaper)

(place on fold)

ANGEL GOWN
(cut 1 from
folded wallpaper)

(place on fold)

**Wallpaper
Angel
pg. 22**

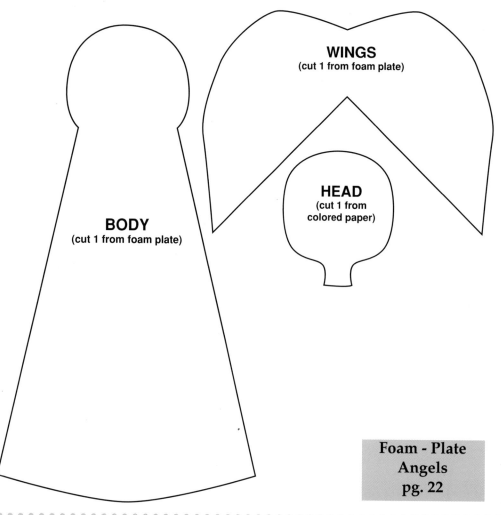

BODY
(cut 1 from foam plate)

WINGS
(cut 1 from foam plate)

HEAD
(cut 1 from
colored paper)

**TIE
KNOT**
(cut 1 from
orange felt)

FEATHERS
(cut 4 from
yellow felt)

BOWTIE

(cut 1 from
orange felt)

BEAK

(cut 1 from
orange felt)

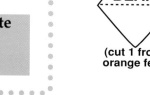

Foam - Plate
Angels
pg. 22

Tissue -
Paper
Tongues of
Fire
pg. 30

Pop - Bottle
Flower Frame
pg. 32

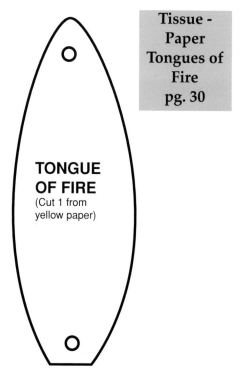

○

**TONGUE
OF FIRE**
(Cut 1 from
yellow paper)

○

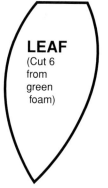

LEAF
(Cut 6
from
green
foam)

FOOT

(cut 2 from
orange felt)

WINGS
(cut 2 from
yellow felt)

Pop-Pom
Easter Chicks
pg. 26

**PAPIER MÂCHÈ
PUPPET COSTUME**
(cut 2 from folded fabric)

(place on fold of fabric)

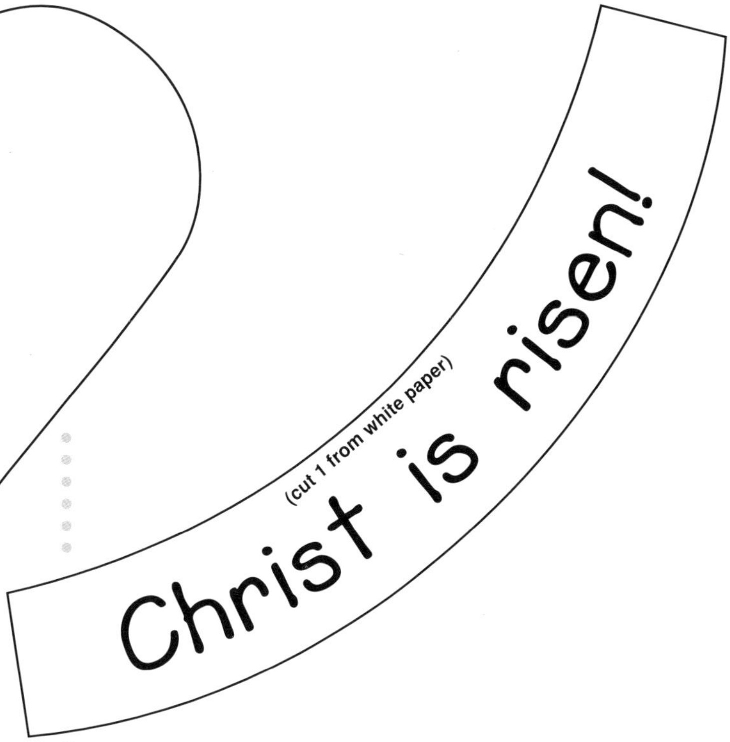

(cut 1 from white paper)

Christ is risen!

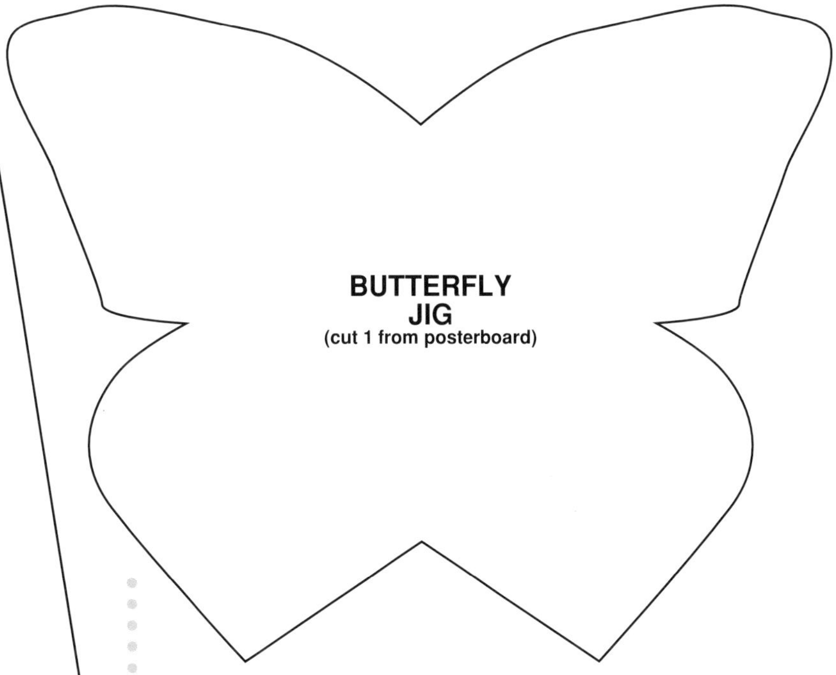

**BUTTERFLY
JIG**
(cut 1 from posterboard)

**Papier Mâché
Puppets
pg. 11**

**Butterfly
Easter Plaque
pg. 26**

Tried-and-True Tips for Group Crafting

• When using glue, keep several damp kitchen sponges on the crafting tables. Children can use these to rub glue off their fingers as they work. This is an especially useful way to encourage children who don't like to get their hands sticky!

• To help younger crafters control the amount of glue they use, pour a little into a small cap (like those found on milk bottles) and show them how to spread the glue with a cotton swab. Again, this is a handy way to encourage those neat crafters who don't like sticky fingers!

• Keep glitter from overtaking your room by showing the children how to hold their projects over a shoe box lid while sprinkling the glitter. When they are done glittering, they can gently tilt the box lid to collect the glitter into the corner and pour it back into the glitter bottle. This is a nice way to conserve glitter, too!

• To keep items the children are painting from sticking to their work surface, have them set the painted items on a sheet of wax paper or on a disposable plastic table cloth. Leave the painted items on the wax paper or tablecloth to dry. When the pieces are thoroughly dry, the children can easily lift them from the surface.

• Instead of buying lots of different colors of paint, consider purchasing only red, blue, yellow, white, and black. From these children can mix all the colors they may need (paper plates make great paint palettes). Even the youngest children will enjoy this activity. Start them with two colors at a time, e.g. red and yellow, and let them see what happens when they mix them.

• Pair younger or inexperienced crafters with older or more experienced ones. Both will benefit from this cooperative arrangement.

• If you are working with many children on a somewhat involved project, make up kits and put all the pieces in a baggie for each child. This may involve some preparation on your part, such as cutting ribbons or yarn to specific lengths, but your extra time will insure more fun and less frustration for you and the children!

Where To Find It

Not-So-Hot Craft Foam Wreath, p. 15 and Noah's Ark, p. 5. To locate Craftfoam Glue from the Beacon Chemical Co. call their customer service number, 1-800-TO-KRAFT.

Pine-Cone Nativity, p. 21. Miniature nativity figures can be ordered from Cousin Coporation of America at 1-800-366-2687 or Craft King at 1-800-769-9494.

Prayer Journal, p. 33. Stiffened Eazy Felt is available from Consumer Products Enterprises, Inc., 1-800-327-0059.